Copyright © 2019 Alli Koch

Published by Blue Star Press
Paige Tate & Co. is an imprint of Blue Star Press
PO Box 5622, Bend, OR 97708
contact@paigetate.com
www.paigetate.com

Illustrations by Alli Koch

ISBN: 978-1944515898

Printed in China

10 9 8 7 6 5 4

Sometimes coloring books can be intimidating rather than relaxing. Flipping through each page, you think how could you ever touch it, fearing you might mess up. I get it. I'm that person! Always just looking and never actually coloring in my books. So I wanted to give you a page to let that fear go. Practice with your materials, clear your head, and just go for it! If you actually loved what you practiced, good! You'll see these elements again throughout this book. Happy coloring!

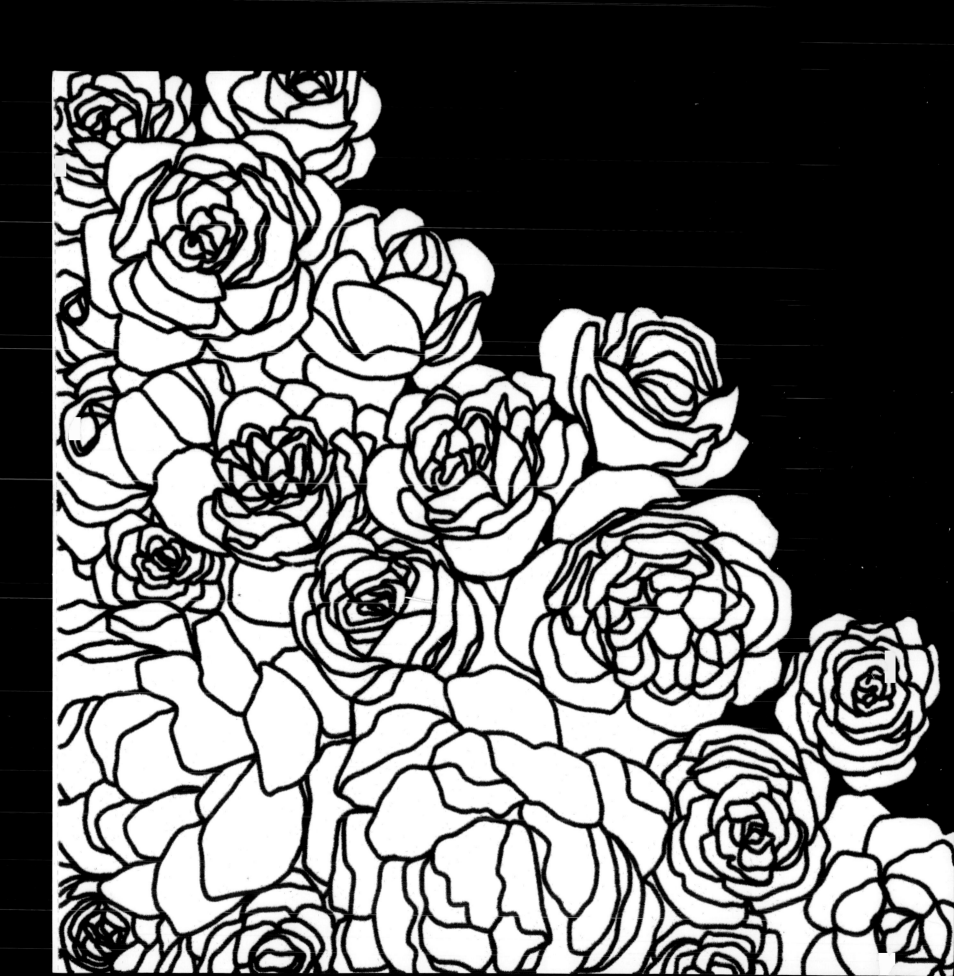

Thank you so much for choosing to invest time in my book and its pages. As an artist, I frequently find myself doodling to release stress and get my creative juices flowing again. Never, in a million years, could I have imagined people using my artwork to do the same. It's such an honor to be able to share my artwork with you. I cannot wait to see how you transform it and customize it to make it completely your own. If you decide to post your work to social media, be sure to use #alwaysbeblooming so that I can see!

Xo, Alli

Alli Koch is the hands and heart behind Alli K Design. She has created a name for herself using her unique drawing style and staple black-and-white color palette. As a visual artist and illustrator, Alli is on a mission to inspire others to create beautiful things. This has led her to publishing two books, *How to Draw Modern Florals* and *Florals by Hand*, which teach readers step-by-step how to draw flowers and cacti, as well as recording a weekly podcast with her dad called *Breakfast with Sis*. When she is not out painting murals around her hometown of Dallas, Texas, you can find Alli in her studio drinking a Chick-fil-A sweet tea and cuddling with her cats. To find out more about Alli and her work, visit www.AlliKDesign.com